Walks from Your Ca

C000090960

Lower
Wharfedale
including the Washburn Valley

by
Geoffrey White and Norman Hancock

Dalesman Books
1990

THE DALESMAN PUBLISHING COMPANY LTD.,
CLAPHAM, via Lancaster, LA2 8EB

First published 1990

ISBN: 0 85206 994 4

Printed byPeter Fretwell & Sons Ltd., Keighley, West Yorkshire BD21 1PZ

Contents

Map on page 11 by Donald Hancock; other maps by Geoffrey White. Drawings by Geoffrey Green.

The authors wish to thank Geoffrey Green and David Nunns for their assistance with this book.

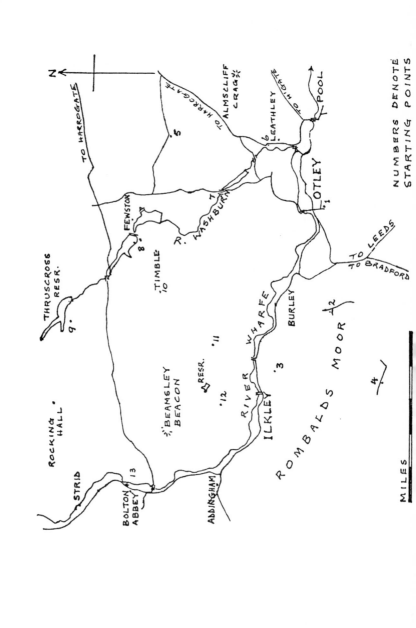

N

MILES

NUMBERS DENOTE
STARTING POINTS

Foreword

QUEEN of the Dales, as Wharfedale is known throughout Yorkshire and England, is truly worthy of that title and amply justifies the locals' intense pride in her. But it appears that most people think only of Bolton Bridge to the river's source, the 'upper reaches', a veritable paradise indeed, but by no means all the story; the river does not terminate, as it were, at Bolton Abbey!

South-east from here, entering almost a different kind of world, the Wharfe sedately twists and turns its lower reaches, joining the Ouse through a more pastoral and, in parts, semi-urban vale, set within a moorland area so ready of access that it long ago became the playground for 'the folk just over the brow' in adjoining Airedale and the West Riding.

This book is another proof of the authors' now well-known gift for sensing those elements of charm and beauty which so often lie in otherwise neglected countryside. Not only have they found the paths and ways which tend to escape the notice of the multitude, or those without eyes to see; but they have astutely included, and given due weight to, such famous features as the Cow and Calf rocks, Otley Chevin, and Bolton Priory and have not failed to touch upon history in the form, for example, of ancient but very significant packtracks like Badgers Gate; all without detracting from the worth and interest of the remainder. Indeed, upon further reflection, it is quite a feat to have found thirteen notably good walks in a mere fifteen miles of dale, embracing within it no less than seven reservoirs.

Though never far from built-up areas and almost within hearing of West Riding industry, this lovely little piece of England has been shown to possess all that the walker desires: beauty, remoteness, wild moorland, easy ascents, and withal a quiet restfulness, so that I can assure the reader of much pleasure in store for him.

Geoffrey Green

Introduction

THIS book is a successor to *Walks in Lower Wharfedale* by Geoffrey White (1980).

'Lower' or 'Middle' Wharfedale? Those who would include in the Dale the country beside the Wharfe as it wanders through the Vale of York would probably call the area covered by this book 'Middle'. Those who consider the end of the Dale to be at the fringe of the hills no doubt think, with us, that the Dale becomes 'Lower' at Bolton Abbey. Probably all agree that Upper Wharfedale is upstream from that village. On a clear day stand above the Cow and Calf rocks, then on Beamsley Beacon, and you will have looked over the whole of the area covered in these pages.

Many books have been written about the Yorkshire Dales including all parts of Wharfedale — the most popular of them all. Nevertheless, we are sure there is a need for a little book concentrating on Lower Wharfedale and the Washburn, not to cover every mile of public footpath but taking walkers new to the district into all parts of it and, perhaps for the 'regulars', giving some variety to well-known walks. In making a selection, we particularly acknowledge the value of the relevant pages in *Striding Through Yorkshire* by A. J. Brown (Country Life Ltd.), now, sadly, out of print.

The proximity of the Dale to the populated areas around Leeds and Bradford means it can be visited on summer evenings or winter afternoons for fresh air, exercise and beauty. For this reason, most of the walks have been kept short, but extensions could be made into longer expeditions. For instance, many variations and additions could be made to Walks 2, 3 and 4 on Rombalds Moor. Footpaths in the Washburn Valley and surrounding moors are legion and 'should keep a man busy for half a year' according to A. J. Brown. An excellent full day on the moors leading to Beamsley Beacon could start at Ilkley or Winds Over Farm gate or Moorside, north of Denton, using some of the tracks taken on Walks 10 to 13. Bolton Abbey is a suitable starting point for more walks, two of which are included in *Walking in the Craven Dales,* a Dalesman Mini-Book by Colin Speakman.

Only one of our chapters includes a stretch beside the River Wharfe, but other waterside walks are easily found, scarcely warranting detailed description; for example between Bolton Bridge and Bolton Priory, as well as the western path mentioned in Walk 13, there is also one on the eastern side giving fine views of the river and the wooded surroundings. A simple circuit suggests itself here. Between the Old Bridge at Ilkley and the village of Addingham is a pleasant walk on the south-western side of the river, this being the beginning of the Dales Way, the long distance walk devised by the Ramblers' Association, West Riding Area, finishing at Bowness-on-Windermere. Another riverside path is on the north side of the Wharfe between Otley and Leathley Bridge; from the Leathley/Pool road a short cut could then be made through the fields to Pool Bridge. The bridge below Harewood on the Harrogate road is another from which footpaths emanate — westwards to Weeton and eastwards to Netherby. On the other side a continuous path reaches the Harewood Avenue Road near its junction with the road to East Keswick. Between Wetherby and Thorp Arch are tracks which touch the riverside near Flintmill Grange. Attractive paths go out from the narrow bridge at Boston Spa south of the river for about a mile each way. For a peaceful stroll on a summer evening, none could be better than to follow the Wharfe gently winding its way from Newton Kyme (a delightful little village) to Tadcaster.

All the walks described in the following chapters are circular — useful when one has to return to a car. They are on rights-of-way except when they are on open moor — then it is made clear when a public path is left. On Ilkley Moor there is full freedom of access and on Burley Moor full access for eight months of the year and limited access for four months of the year. Access agreements are in force on the moors controlled by the Chatsworth Estate Company (Walks 9 and 13). During the shooting season the moors are closed on certain week days, notices being posted at points of entry well in advance of the closure. On other moors, crossed by rights-of-way, the reader is advised to give guns a wide berth.

The map for each walk is intended only as a guide and the walker is recommended to use, in addition, the Ordnance Survey Map No. 104, 1:50,000 scale or SE 04/14 and SE 05/15 of the Pathfinder range, 1:25000 scale. It is sometimes useful to carry a compass and, very often, a waterproof. Some of the gentler walks could be done wearing ordinary clothing and strong footwear, but the wilder places merit the wearing of walking boots, thick socks (perhaps more than one pair), warm clothing, anorak and a rucksack with some food and a vacuum flask.

Here is a list of our favourite walks in the different sections of the area. It may help you to decide which ones to select first.

But wait — Timble, Almscliff Crag and Rocking Hall are missing: it may be that, on second thoughts, you will just have to work steadily through them all. Geoffrey White confesses he included Walk 7 for sentimental reasons. Sixty years ago he enjoyed being a member of the 'Wayfarers', a cheerful and vigorous rambling club. From time to time they would visit the Washburn and on one occasion a press photographer was waiting for any hikers who might be coming that way at Dobpark Bridge. He still has a copy of the picture which appeared in the old *Leeds Mercury* to remind him of some of his happiest days. His wife (though not then married) was a member — so was Geoffrey Green. At the same time Norman Hancock enjoyed many years of cycling and walking throughout the whole area covered by the book, with many happy memories. May future generations be so blest.

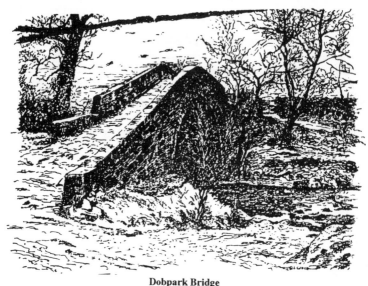

Dobpark Bridge

Otley Chevin

MANY people have had their first view of Lower Wharfedale from this well-known beauty spot. The grounds of Danefield Estate offer tracks galore through delightful woodland, parkland and picnic places, and are liberally supplied with footpath maps which should help the walker to vary at will the suggested route.

Parking: GR:217443 marked by a footpath and bridleway sign opposite York Gate Farm on East Chevin Road.

The car park gives access to the Chevin Forest Park, named here as Shawfield, and there is a large notice board with a helpful map. Go to the left of the notice board (the track to the right of it comes down from the upper of two car parks) to join the track named as Chippendale Ride. At this point there is a commemorative post for a tree given by the Queen, recording the birth of Thomas Chippendale in Otley in 1718, also a large stone slab reminding us that the maker of fine furniture lived in Otley.

Pass through some grand common ground with picnic tables among the trees, and proceed along a well laid-out track, with seats and with occasional vistas through the trees towards the Washburn Valley. Finally you walk past a large memorial stone, a few paces into the wood on the right, beyond which, at the end of the wood on the left, you turn downhill on a stony road. The area on the right, known as Caley Deer Park, has been planted with conifers.

At the next junction, note at the corner of the bridleway a large isolated stone pillar. At this point it is worth turning right for 170 yards to stand on the top of Caley Crags and to admire the magnificent view; but our walk turns left at the stone pillar and continues forward with woods on the left and open views of Wharfedale on the right. At a clear area, with a picnic table, a marker post and two groups of birch trees, take the lower track below the crags (unless you wish to return early to the car park — in which case go straight on). The rocks on this lower track are quite impressive and are obviously used as a climbing ground. Farnley Hall should be seen across the valley as well as the radio mast on Norwood Edge, and

Almscliff Crag should be in sight to the right of it.

Enter the woods and note a track going down right, which goes to Holbeck Gate on the Leeds road; a track going upwards at this point is another route back to the car park. Our route, however, goes straight on and crosses a sylvan ravine with a stream below, to reach a group of maintenance buildings. Now the track takes us through a woodland area with some seats and picnic tables, and a waterfall up the hill on the left. With increasing noise of traffic we join the public road, emerging at Danefield gate with a notice board and map. There is also a large round stone which has a notice affixed indicating that this is the Danefield Estate.

Up the road to the left are the two car parks from which we started, and to which some may wish to return. If this is so, proceed with caution keeping well to the side and, about halfway up the hill, divert into the wood, at a stile, and continue parallel to the road.

To complete the full walk, with still much interest to come, walk up the road for a few yards only and note, on the right, the East Chevin Quarry car park. This is at GR:212445 and the full circular walk could start from here if required. Cross the road and go through the car park to another notice board and map. Now we are on a track along the hillside, passing many rocks and cliffs on the left, Pelstone Crag, and with wide-ranging open views of Wharfedale on the right. There are seats and picnic tables which provide an opportunity to rest and admire the valley views, or from which to explore this delightful area. A little further on there is also an opportunity to call at a Visitor Centre and Tea Room.

Continue along the track and, shortly after it enters woodland, take a sharp turn up to the left and then right. We are now almost up the hill and walking parallel to the skyline, and will shortly reach a point where stone steps go steeply down right. These steps would also take you down to the Visitor Centre, returning to this point from there. However, we turn left up a short narrow path which takes us up to the top.

This is "Top of the Chevin", and here we turn left (eastwards) and continue along a wide path and wallside, to join a lane taking us down to the main road. Cross the road, with care, and go into the woods through a stile in the wall immediately opposite. Turn right on an uphill path, parallel to the road, which takes you through the woods back to the car park.

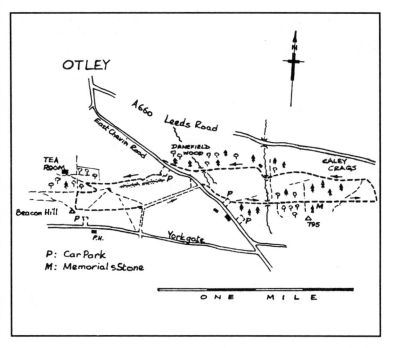

OTLEY

A660 Leeds Road

East Chevin Road

DANEFIELD WOOD

TEA ROOM

CALEY CRAGS

Beacon Hill

Yorkgate

P.H.

P: Car Park
M: Memorials Stone

ONE MILE

However, at the "Top of the Chevin" there is an opportunity to delay departure from this interesting area and to wander at will along the top, with further extensive views over the Wharfe valley, returning always to the gateway at which we arrived. There is also a large car park, which is at GR:205440, and this is yet another place from which the full circular walk could start. Also by crossing the car park to the road one could visit the Royalty Hotel for refreshment if desired.

2.   **5 miles**

Cow and Calf Rocks and Burley Moor

THERE are paths and tracks in abundance on Ilkley and Burley Moors. So many, perhaps, that they become confusing, and it is sometimes difficult to maintain an intended direction. The area has many interesting possibilities and a good map will enable the walker to arrange his or her own way according to inclination and ability. Our intention has been to suggest an interesting and exhilarating route which should be followed without too much difficulty. Remember always that these moors can be dangerous in bad weather, and that conditions can sometimes change very dramatically and very quickly.

Parking: GR:133467. One and a half miles out of Ilkley, on the moor road to Bingley and Guiseley, are the famous Cow and Calf rocks, where there is ample accommodation for the parking of cars.

From the car park, ascend to the left of the rocks, at first on a stepped path and then, bearing slightly left, keep upwards on one of several paths to join a wide stony track coming up from the Cow and Calf Hotel. Continue up the moor and, at the first ridge, turn left along the moor edge.

There is now about a mile of fine moorland and walking along a good track to reach the ravine Cold Stone Beck. This section provides extensive views of the lower Wharfe valley; over on the left will be seen the landmarks of the radio mast on Norwood Edge, Almscliff Crag, Otley Chevin and — on very clear days — York Minster beyond. This track over Stead Crags is the old main route between Ilkley and Menston/Baildon. The track now traverses the ravine and climbs up the other side where it forks. Keep to the upper route which passes to the right of a quarry and two farms at Crag Top. Now with a wall on the left continue past York View Farm and follow the wall round under the reservoir dam — this is Carr Bottom Reservoir. The track rises up to reach another main moorland track near a square brick building, now disused. This ancient route has been known locally as the Gaping Goose (or 'Intake Gate') track.

Now make an acute turn to the right, and proceed up the moor on a good track. This is Burley Moor and nearby is a notice indicating that dogs must be kept on leash. There are two sources of danger; one is from the nearby rifle range and the other is in the grouse shooting season. Both may be easily avoided by careful observation of notices displayed on the moor, especially during the shooting season when some routes may be closed. Another danger is to the birds during the nesting season, but walkers keeping to the indicated routes are within

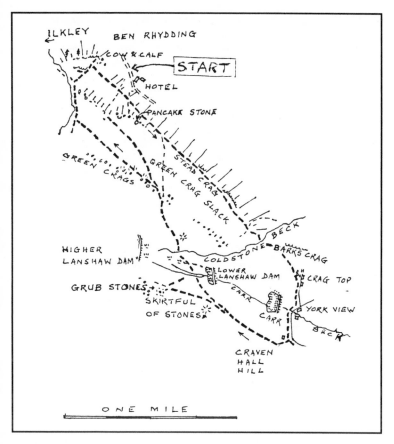

their rights.

Continuing on the main track there will first be a sight of the lower reservoir, Carr Bottom Reservoir, then of the second reservoir, Lower Lanshaw Dam. It is about here that the right-of-way, a faint track through heather, leaves the main track to pass over two arms of Carr Beck on a stone slab and a plank bridge to go up to the Little Skirtful of Stones, seen as a cairn on the skyline in front.

If it is not the shooting season, an easier and more rewarding route is to continue up the main track, passing to the left of a flagstaff and to the right of a vehicle park for private shoots. Leave the main track to go up to the rocks — The Grub Stones — for a good general view of Rombalds Moor and the Aire valley beyond in the Keighley, Bingley and Shipley region.

Off the track are also the cairn, Big Skirtful of Stones, and a stone circle. Return to the main track and pick up a clear footpath through the heather, going back to the crossings of the Carr Beck.

Bear left on the other side of the beck and the path continues on raised ground beside the stream and through marshy land. Cross the stream and continue on a green track through the heather to the left of the tumulus above — Little Skirtful of Stones — a hollowed-out cairn of small stones. The single track is quite apparent as you round the cairn, but not so easily seen further on. It is useful to walk on a compass bearing of 320 degrees. A good marker is a signpost beside some rocks (Green Crags). Good tracks cross Green Crag Slack, either to join the outward route above Stead Crag, or to arrive at the cup and ring marked rocks above the Cow and Calf hotel.

For the variety of a more circuitous route, however, keep to the ridge and the rocks of Green Crags until you reach a second group of stones on a clear path in single file and go onwards, as it slopes downhill. From here there are views of Middleton across the Wharfe from Ilkley, March Ghyll Reservoir beyond it, and Beamsley Beacon. Continue towards the stream and turn right on a good path just before it, keeping near the right bank of the beck which flows into a conduit and then bounds over rocks down to the junction of several tracks, the one to the left leading to Rocky Valley below Ilkley Crags. Do not cross the stream but go forward over the plain towards rocks and conifers ahead — Hanging Stones, more popularly known as the Cow and Calf (the calf being the enormous boulder below, not yet in sight). Parts of Ilkley will be seen on the left and there will be a glimpse of the tarn below. Walk along the lip of an old quarry and suddenly you arrive at one of Yorkshire's most famous viewpoints embracing almost the whole of the area covered by this book.

Ilkley Moor

VIEWS from, and places of interest, the edge of the moor above Ilkley make any walk or stroll along it rewarding. Distances may be adjusted according to one's inclination: today's full walk as illustrated on the sketch map may be reduced by more than a mile by making one's way down to the Swastika Stone when it is in sight. There are no restrictions as regards the footpaths on the Ilkley Moor part of Rombalds Moor, but there are so many tracks to assist the walker that it is unnecessary to depart from them, and it is undesirable in the nesting season. The walk may be extended along the edge — say to Windgate Nick, which is a mile away from the illustrated turning-point.

Parking: The car park is between the Cow and Calf Rocks and the hotel, (GR:133467).

Walk up the main track to the cliffs — Hanging Stones, a great rock climbing area — passing to the left of them for an easy ascent to the top where, no doubt, there will be a pause for the view. Now curve away from the rocks on a main path, to pass another quarry basin on the right, and head up on a clear path to cross a tumbling stream on rocks. The main path on the other side goes below the crags and through Rocky Valley. We shall take that route to this point on our return. Now we turn upwards on a good track to Ilkley Crags, and walk along the top edge of Rocky Valley to a large cairn, which marks the junction with a main path coming down from the top of the moor. This is Cranshaw Thorn Hill from which White Wells will be seen below and almost the whole of Ilkley, with Addingham ahead and Beamsley Beacon to the right, beyond the Wharfe. Soon, take the upper of two tracks (temporarily towards two pylons on the skyline) and again an upper path which soon levels out after avoiding marshy land, the masts now being more on our left. About three-quarters of a mile from the last big cairn, the track bends left to descend into the valley for the crossing of the two heads of the next stream, at Wicken Tree Crag. Here a diversion square to the left for 150 yards over the moor brings us to a memorial seat at the Badger Stone, a reclining rock on which concentric rings are marked — the

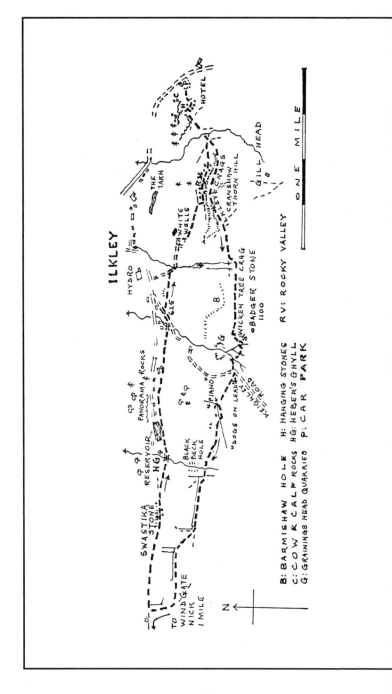

ILKLEY

B: BARMISHAW HOLE   H: HANGING STONES   RV: ROCKY VALLEY
C: COW & CALF ROCKS   HG: HEBER'S GHYLL
G: GRAININGS HEAD QUARRIES   P: CAR PARK

ONE MILE

ancient cup and ring marks found on so many of the stones on these moors. Return to the path crossing Grainings Head and continue on the other side of the two stream crossings, on a clear path through bracken to the metalled, but not tarred, Keighley Road, at a bend above a sharp gradient.

Go up the road for a few yards, and continue in the line of march on a track which passes between two short tree trunk posts and make for the rocks on Coarse Stone Edge, one of which looks like an open grand piano; on it is 'Dogs on lead' notice. From now on, the views on the right include much of Upper Wharfedale, including Earl Seat and Simon's Seat and Burnsall and Thorpe Fell. Continue forward, with a wall over to the left, on a well defined path, and cross a shallow depression to the next stream at a point above Black Beck Hole. The little beck is easily crossed on rocks. Go through a gap in the wall ahead and continue on the track to the left of a wall which ends near a solitary boulder. The Swastika Stone, protected by railings, should be seen from all sections of this wall and those not wishing to complete the full circuit could make their way down to it. Otherwise, continue beyond the end of the wall and gradually slope down to the head of a narrow intake between stone walls and continue on good tracks through grass or heather on the left of a wall at first, then across heather to join a wide track which has sloped down from the moor edge on the left. Follow it downhill to the left of a wall when soon you will join a very clear cairned track.

If you wish to extend the walk for another mile each way, turn left and follow the cairns on a track which keeps to the moor edge and passes through stiles in crossing walls. This takes you above the crags on the edge of Addingham High Moor and to Windgate Nick, identified when you reach a narrow cross track coming from a stile to the left front and going down a gap in the rocks below. White Crag Plantation can be seen ahead. Return to the cairns where the circuit was left and go straight on.

Those not wishing to extend the circuit should turn right at the cairns and follow a clear track for half a mile, losing a little height to reach the Swastika Stone in a rocky area. A plaque, below the carving on the rock of a rounded version of the ancient sign adopted by the Nazis, tells us that it was probably a good luck symbol and dates from the Bronze Age. Similar signs have been found in Sweden and in Greece. Continuing towards Ilkley, keep to a lower track which passes to the head of the woods near Heber's Ghyll, then cross the rushing stream on the top footbridge, from which others may be seen below, to pass alongside the oblong reservoir on a clear footpath. Go over a delightful rocky stream and reach a tarmac road. Walk downhill on the road for a hundred yards and turn right on a rough track across the moor to join a wide rocky road. Turn right and go uphill to White Wells (open to the public). The road becomes a track sloping up through a nick. If you pause at White Wells, make sure you resume the upward route of the original track. Where it forks beneath a series of stone steps, bear left and very soon you enter the Rocky Valley, boulder-strewn and close beneath Ilkley Crags, and well worth the effort As you emerge, you can see the clear path on the left, returning to the outward track at the stream crossing. Now it is simply a matter of retracing your steps to the Hanging Stones and the Cow and Calf car park below.

4.
                                     'A' route: 8 miles
                                    'B' route: 4.25 miles

Dick Hudson's to Ilkley

MANY tracks over Rombalds Moor connect Airedale with Wharfedale, and the one selected for today is the most famous of them all, starting from the well-known pub, named *Dick Hudson's,* at the junction of the Eldwick/Bingley road with the moor road connecting Morton with Menston and Ilkley. 'B' route is for motorists beginning their walk at Whetstone Gate, (GR:102453), reached by car from the crossroads half a mile west of West Morton. The surface between the gate and Ilkley is unfit for ordinary cars.

Parking: Route 'A' starts from the oven door stile, (GR:124422). If you are not a pub customer, there is room for parking round the corner on the verge.

The path immediately enters a double-walled gulley. Eldwick Crag is on the left. Leave the lane through a stile and continue forward, with a post and wire fence on your right. Passing through a little iron gate, join a stone trod dropping down to Weecher Mouth where the track becomes stony, then wide, as it passes through bog, but it then becomes dry again on its upward trail over Hog Hill, with Wicking Crag Stones on the right. So far, we have been on Bingley Moor but, on crossing the parish wall on a stone step stile the public path crosses a corner of Burley Moor before Ilkley Moor is joined at Lanshaw Lad, a little more than half a mile ahead. Pass a leaning stone guide-post and, after passing two single foot tracks on the right, nearly at the top of the ridge where a big cairn (Lanshaw Lad) will be seen ahead, a stone circle is just off the track on the right. Fifty feet in diameter, it comprises twelve major upright stones — the Twelve Apostles. 'B' walkers may join the route at Lanshaw Lad — or just to the north of it — and the outlook from the ridge is pleasing. Nearby on the left is the trig point, 1,320 feet, on White Crag Moss; the rocks of Lanshaw Delves on the right will soon come into sight; further afield are the moors beyond Ilkley, including Beamsley Beacon. An extensive board walk assists the crossing of marshy land before arriving at Gill Head. Keep straight on, using the main cairned track which skirts Cranshaw Thorn Hill, as far as a big heap of stones where the path described in Walk 3 — over Ilkley Crags — crosses from right to left. Pause to admire the view of Ilkley and beyond and here decide which of several alternatives to choose. You could keep along the top as far as the Keighley Road, as described in Walk 3; or you could go into Ilkley and, later, join the Keighley Road; or you could take a variety of middle courses, one of which will now be described.

The track descends steeply towards White Wells. Before going down a stone stairway, a visit to the edge would be rewarded by views of Rocky Valley and Hanging Stones beyond. Assisted by the steps, there is a quick descent to White Wells (open to the public). Return uphill for a little way and take one of several paths on the right which lead upwards towards a copse in a ravine. Continue to the top and join another track aiming towards a fir tree plantation, from the top corner of which a single track continues towards Grainings Head Quarries (disused). Descend to the quarry floor and pick up a clear path which crosses the stream, then ascend to a path going forward to the rough Keighley road. Follow the road up to the television masts, passing Cowper's Cross on the way. The gate across the road, near the masts, is Whetstone Gate — where 'B' walkers pick up the circuit.

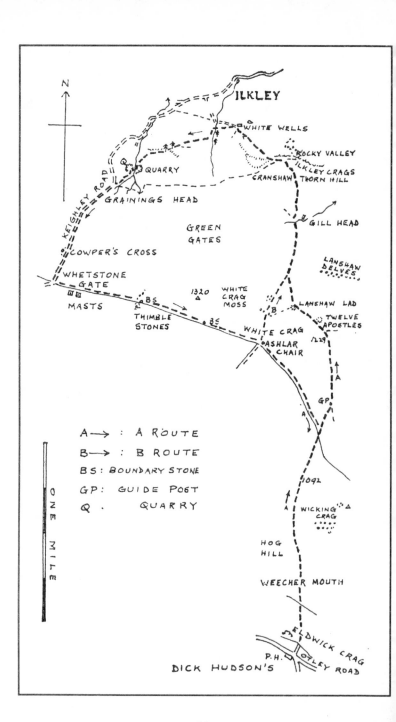

N

ILKLEY

WHITE WELLS

ROCKY VALLEY
ILKLEY CRAGS
THORN HILL
CRANSHAW

QUARRY

KEIGHLEY ROAD

GRAININGS HEAD

GREEN
GATES

GILL HEAD

COWPER'S CROSS

LANSHAW
DELVES

WHETSTONE
GATE

1320

WHITE
CRAG
MOSS

LANSHAW LAD

MASTS

BS

B

TWELVE
APOSTLES

THIMBLE
STONES

BS

WHITE CRAG

1229

ASHLAR
CHAIR

A

GP

A

A — : A ROUTE

B — : B ROUTE

BS : BOUNDARY STONE

GP : GUIDE POST

Q . QUARRY

1092

A

WICKING
CRAG

HOG
HILL

ONE MILE

WEECHER MOUTH

ELDWICK CRAG

P.H.

OTLEY ROAD

DICK HUDSON'S

20

The wall is again the parish boundary. To the north of it is Ilkley Moor; to the south, Morton Moor. It is on the Ilkley side that the much-walked track is taken, at first through half a mile of marshy moor to the wrinkled, gritty, Thimble Stones. Continue by the wall side to Ashlar Chair, situated at a turning of the wall. Here is a collection of more than a dozen large stones, the biggest of which has chair-like hollows in it. A footpath from East Morton crosses here, coming through a stile in the wall, and continues towards Ilkley to join the Dick Hudson track after passing through the rocks of White Crag and, maybe, diverting right for Lanshaw Lad. This is the 'B' route.

Walkers on the 'A' trail keep straight on, where they will find good use made of the wall as shooting butts, with platforms over the ditch to each butt. The next stone step stile in the wall should be recognised from the outward journey. Go over it and, on a wide track taking you away from the wall, return to *Dick Hudson's.*

5.   **8.75 miles**

Almscliff Crag
and Little Almscliff

THE charm of these two famous outcrops of millstone grit is first their association with famous mountaineers — notably Smythe — who used the cracks and chimneys of the Great Crag as a climbing training area; secondly, they are landmarks for miles around and, conversely, fine viewpoints for Lower Wharfedale, Ilkley Moor, Otley Chevin and the Arthington Viaduct — and beyond to the Wolds, Hambletons and the White Horse, and even York Minster, providing the weather conditions are clear. The pylon to the west of the Little Crag is the radio mast on Norwood Edge and the water seen to the north of this Little Almscliff (or Almias Cliff), is Scargill Reservoir. A third interest is in the legends associated with the rocks: Orm was a landowner living here in the olden days, the spelling of his name giving the clue to the usual pronunciation of the cliff names; there is also a Lovers' Leap. Finally, the walk over Lindley and Stainburn Moors provides an invigorating and rewarding link between the Crags.

Parking: For the convenience of motorists' car parking, the walk is shown as starting from the north but motorists who wish to park near the Great Crag (GR:265492), joining the route there, will have to be content with parking on the verge of the narrow lanes. On the Beckwithshaw to Bland Hill (Norwood) road, about two miles from Beckwithshaw, there is a Forestry Commission car park — Stainburn Moor (GR:235524), Knaresborough Forest — at a sharp bend.

Walk up the road for 300 yards to a gate on the left and the track to Little Almscliff. Explore the rocks, admire the scene and return to the car park, and from there go through the main gate into the forest and forward on the main forest road. Emerging from the wood, the road takes an abrupt turn to the right, but leave it here and go forward to a gate to continue in the same direction, with a fence on the left following the line of a deep-cut drain. The fence turns away to the left, but keep straight on over the moor on a path that varies, sometimes on a raised walk, sometimes a shallow ditch alongside, sometimes a wide cart track. Go through a gate at a wall corner and cross West Beck on stepping stones and continue on a green track with a good wall on the left and a dilapidated one on the right, over Napes Hill and through a gate into a good cart lane which becomes tarred before emerging on to the B6161. Keep straight on, passing Hill Top farm, but leave it to take the tarmac lane on the left. Pass a drive and a pair of cottages and bear left before the farm seen ahead to cross West Beck on a substantial bridge in a pleasant setting. The leafy lane uphill joins the narrow road in the village of Braythorn at an old chapel. Turn right and walk down the road to the church and use the footpath through the churchyard only as far as the porch.

Here the splendid views include one of Almscliff Crag, seen beyond the east end of the church. Go towards it on a grass path and climb a stile, formerly a gate, crossing the field roughly parallel to the wall on the left. Then go down to a stile to the left of a hen hut, continue over the beck on a stone footbridge — partly demolished but crossable with care — and cross the fence at an old stone stile. Walk up the right-hand side of the fence, hedge and wall, pass to the left of a barn and bear half-right from the wall to a footpath sign beside a stile to the public

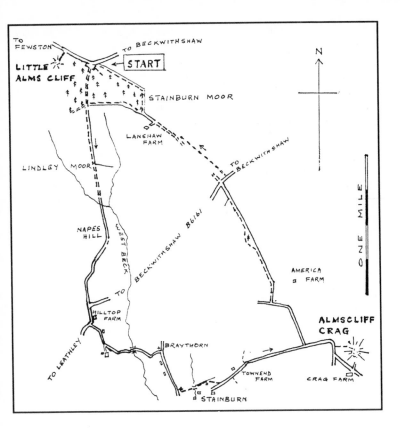

road. (This diversion from the church has reduced a little of the amount of road walking, but a straightforward alternative would be to keep to the tarmac path through the churchyard, cut to the left-hand bottom corner of the field and turn left on the road to pass through the village of Stainburn.) The crag is now a mile away by narrow road. Just beyond the sharp bend at the end of the straight stretch, go over a stone stile at a footpath sign and, on a path to the right of a wall, enter, through a gate, the area of Almscliff Crag.

The return route is down to the road again, retrace your steps to the first road junction on the right, turn on to it (signposted Leathley two-and-a-half), take the next bend to the left and go over a stile 250 yards ahead at a public bridleway signpost. The track keeps to the left of a wire fence on rough grazing land, to the left of a new plantation and back to the fence, and passes through gates, keeping fences and walls on the right and finally to a lane with fences on both sides and an enclosure and a radio mast on the left. Pass through a wide gateway on to the public road and turn right. Then walk with care along the road for 250 yards as far as Briscoerigg Farm. The right-of-way track to Stainmoor starts at the left hand of two gates on the left, opposite the farm.

Go through the gate into a small field and walk on a grass track beside a wall and fence on the right, with a very fine view over the valley in which the River Crimple starts. Pass through another gate and walk along a grass lane, which is between a wall and a fence, for about half a mile aiming towards woods on the skyline. Our track finally enters a field, in which there is a gate adjoining the tarmac track bending towards Lanshaw Farm, but our right-of-way goes a little further into the field along the wallside to a stile and footpath sign. After negotiating the stile, turn right and go forward towards the woods on a very wide grass track which may be wet and boggy. Beyond a further gateway bear left alongside the woods of Stainburn Moor to rejoin the outward route, then turn right on the forest road back to the car park.

6.

'A' route: 6 miles
'B' route: 5 miles
Reservoir only: 3.25 miles

Leathley and Lindley Wood Reservoir

THIS popular area includes the lovely, scattered village of Leathley, famous for its church, the lowest of the Washburn reservoirs, set in woodland, and — for route 'A' walkers — the estate village of Farnley where, at the Hall, Turner was a frequent visitor and where he painted many of his pictures.

Parking: For 'A' and 'B' routes, park your car on the plateau opposite Leathley church, (GR:232470), where the views over the lower Wharfe valley are delightful. Those intending to walk the shortest route should start from the small car park, (GR:209499), (where there is room for about ten cars) at the corner of the reservoir bridge, joining 'B' route. If you are in Pool, without a car, it would be easy to join the circuit at Leathley by walking from Pool Bridge across the clearly signposted field paths, adding one-and-a-half miles each way.

Followers of 'A' and 'B' routes walk to Leathley Mill, half a mile north of the church, just before a bend in the narrow road, turn left at a sign 'Public Footpath to Lindley Bridge', passing through two gates and skirting to the right of the old mill building on a clear path. Go over a stile and keep to the path beside the mill race, with the River Washburn down below on the left, fast flowing in a delightful valley. The path soon comes to the riverbank. Follow a sign 'Please keep to the footpath'. At the first bend of the river do not go into the field ahead, instead go uphill to rejoin the Mill Goit, passing trout hatcheries on the way to Lindley Bridge, reached by means of a stone stairway. Route 'B' walkers should note this point for the return journey. 'Reservoir Only' walkers join the circuit here. At the top of the steps turn right to walk along the road for less than 50 yards. Turn left at a sign 'Public Footpath to Norwood Bottom' to walk past a lodge on a wide track through Lindley Wood, which soon reaches the dam and the stepped overflow which gives an impressive roar when in spate. Wild life on the water and the sight of the distant moors provide interest for the next mile beside the reservoir. Turn left to cross the water over the bridge where no doubt you will pause for the view which will include the radio mast at Norwood. The car park on the right at the end of the bridge will be the starting point for some.

For route 'B' there is nearly a mile of road walking, busy with cars at weekends, to the turning-off point which is just past the bend after the long straight stretch of tarmac road. Turn left through a gate at a public footpath sign and follow a grass track in a field with a hedge on your right. Go through a gateway and continue forward, passing the end of the reservoir to join a narrow tarmac road, over a stile beside a gate and a footpath sign. Turn left and walk down the road to Lindley Bridge where 'B' walkers turn right for home and reservoir walkers turn left at the lodge.

Resuming the 'A' journey from the car park at the end of the bridge, walk up the hill and follow the road acutely to the left near the top for about 100 yards beyond Rose Tree Farm. Leave the road squarely on the right at a public footpath sign,

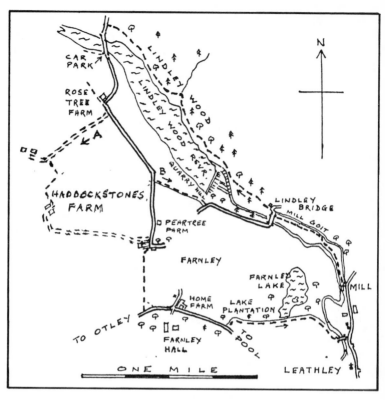

the second of two. Keep on this straight tarmac single road
until, before reaching a sharp turning to the farm seen on the
right, go through a gateway on the left and, with a wall on
the right, keep on a cart track to a gate. Beyond the gate take
a sharp right-turn towards a copse and follow the perimeter
wall of the field as far as a gate marked 'footpath' leading
into the yard of Haddockstones Farm. Passing straight through
the yard, keep to the hard farm road, giving good views of
Lower Wharfedale, as far as All Saints Church.

Go out on to the road, turn right and right again beyond the
church at a gate and footpath sign. Pass through another small
gate on the left, turn right and walk below the level of the
churchyard. Bear left and then go in a straight line, with first
a fence on your right and then a hedge. You are walking over
an old stone trod, part of which will be seen.

Cross over a conduited stream and keep straight ahead still
on the stone trod (the green cart track to the gate on the left

front does not carry a right-of-way). A footpath sign and stile indicate the point of egress on to the Otley Road. Turn left to use the footpath beside the road, passing the road to Norwood and Pateley Bridge on the left and Farnley Hall on the right. Continuing forward, the fine Home Farm buildings are on the left. Walk on the road for a third of a mile, turning off left through a small gate, just before a right-hand bend, at a footpath sign indicating 'To Leathley'.

This final stretch on a field track beside Lake Plantation gives fine views of the wide sweep of Lower Wharfedale with Pool and its paper mills on the right. To the left front, over the trees, is Almscliff Crag. Later, through the trees, there may be a glimpse of Farnley Lake. Leathley is spread out ahead, with the church prominent. The Washburn is joined, flowing below on the left, then crossed on a substantial footbridge and from there you traverse a field to a white gate and ladder stile (signposted) in Leathley, 500 yards south of the mill. Turn right along the road to the car.

7.   4.5 miles

Dobpark Bridge
and Low Snowden

THE most notable feature here today is the ancient packhorse bridge over the River Washburn. its shapely lines in a sylvan setting, beside a ford through the rippling river, have made it a focal point for many generations of ramblers. Our turning-point — Washburn Farm at Low Snowden — is also famous. Here Mrs. Dibbs dispensed tea and affection to thousands of walkers, many of whom she knew by name and most of whom she knew would make considerable deviations from their route in order to partake of her famous teas. She died in the 1960s, aged 96. These delights apart, the whole walk takes in the Washburn Valley at its best, the top end of the Lindley Wood

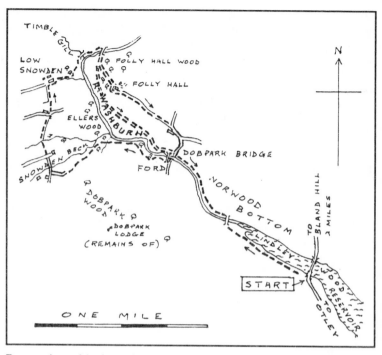

Reservoir, with its wild life, being added as a bonus.

Parking: Three miles north of Otley, on the Pateley Bridge Road, park the car at the southern end of the bridge over Lindley Wood Reservoir where, on the west side of the road, there is space for about ten cars, carefully parked (GR:209498).

A public footpath sign points to a gate and stile and a clear path beside the water. Cross an iron-railed wide bridge and follow the river upstream. Here, in this lovely valley of Norwood Bottom, the river is tree-lined. The hump-backed, pack-horse, Dobpark Bridge is soon reached and crossed. Turn right immediately, over a stile beside a gate, and follow a tractor trail soon taking its somewhat muddy way upwards to a gate. Follow the line of the river, above trees, and enter Ellers Wood by a gate. Go over the stream and bear left upwards, noting a footpath marker on a tree and moving away from the river. On reaching a stile, walk on the right of a wall above Snowden beck, then through the wood to meet a wall on the right, which follow to a fence stile giving access to a narrow lane, initially boggy, and arrive at a cart lane below two farms. Turn right. The lane crosses the stream; at the end of the lane, cross a narrow grass intake (leading down to a ruin) and continue over the next field on the left of power lines to a step stile at the top end of some trees. Bear left to a ladder stile over a wall and follow the wall on your right which takes you round a farm over to the right. Cross the farm track to another ladder stile, cross the field towards the protruding wall corner and go over the ladder stile beside a tree. Go forward on the right of a wall to a stile leading to Washburn Farm.

Turn right to pass in front of the house and to the right of the buildings and make towards the head of a stream, following its left bank to a field where a wood will be seen on the left. Skirt round the bottom of the wood to cross the next field diagonally down to the Washburn, joined by Timble Gill Beck which is crossed by means of another hump-backed bridge. But this one is in miniature — just wide enough to take a boot — and is quite enchanting. It was built of stone from the stream bed by the Ramblers' Association West Riding Area (mainly by Harry Smith) in 1969 in memory of Alderman Arthur Adamson of the City of Leeds, a keen rambler in the early 1920s and until his death. It replaced an earlier bridge washed away. Soon you cross the river on an iron cattle bridge and reverse direction. Follow the good, wide track downstream. After 100 yards, a water supply goes underground. Here make a choice whether to continue on the track through the valley back to Dobpark Bridge, or go uphill on a wide cattle track through Folly Hall Wood for wider views. If taking the latter course, on emerging from the trees, cross a wet field to a gate in the top corner. Pick up a cart track round to the right of Folly Hall. Across the valley will be seen the folly, the ruins of Dobpark Lodge (or Dobpark Castle).

Now on a gated farm track, a wall is first on your left and then on your right, where the road starts gradually to rise. Join a narrow tarmac road at a notice saying 'Folly Hall Wood' and go downhill towards Dobpark Bridge. At the foot of the hill a familiar gate and stile will be seen on the left. Return by the route of the outward journey — Norwood Bottom, then the bridge and lakeside — back to the car.

Timble

TO many ramblers from Leeds and West Yorkshire, whose earliest steps in the countryside were taken in the Washburn Valley, Timble must be a magic name. Its commanding position overlooking the lower Washburn, with Snowden Crags on the right and Norwood Edge on the left — now identified by the high radio mast — and the strategic placement of the *Timble Inn,* combine to remind the walker of happy youthful days. Fewston and Swinsty are more names to evoke memories: this walk should help the old hand to consolidate the images of former days, and the newcomer to store up scenes for future recollection.

Parking: Swinsty Moor car park, (GR:186538), to the south of Fewston reservoir embankment.

Walk back to the car park gates and go to another gate, of the Yorkshire Water Authority, where a notice says: 'Private Road, authorised vehicles only'. Adjoining it is a wicket gate leading to a public footpath. Both tracks go to the first objective — Swinsty Hall — the drive reaching the water first, but the path giving softer going through the trees of Swinsty Moor Plantation, and there are occasional glimpses to the left of Swinsty Reservoir. The radio mast is straight ahead and soon the ancient Swinsty Hall is reached. It is notable for its association with witches and for the legend that its master provided beer in an outside hollow stone for the benefit of the needy during the Plague. Join the lakeside drive by turning left on the road before the house then turn right and walk beside the water to the Swinsty embankment. Cross the road and go through the gate.

Continue on the main drive and if water is rippling down the sluice on the left the sound will be soothing; pass through gates on a farm road in a fine curving river valley, with the Washburn across the fields on the left. On reaching a substantial metal bridge over the river, do not cross but keep to the riverside and go over a stile at the corner of a wall. For a third of a mile this is a reversal of Walk 7, crossing the delightful miniature stone hump-backed bridge over Timble Gill Beck, and going diagonally uphill to pass through the wood ahead, joining the track through it where a fence on the right meets the wood

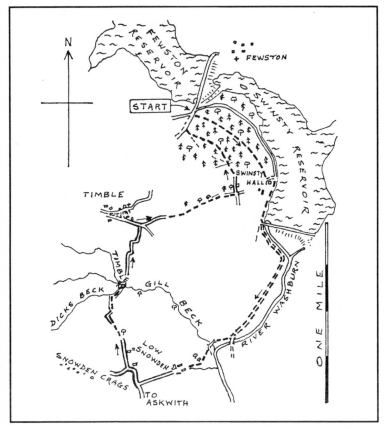

edge. Keep to high ground in the wood to avoid marsh. Continue forward to a lane leading to Washburn Farm at Low Snowden. Pass in front of the house and walk up the road, partly tarred, towards Snowden Crags. Turn right on the narrow motor road, passing a gas main sign in the wood on the left. At the bend just past the first farm, turn right to continue the line of march in a lane, sometimes muddy at first but later becoming grassy. Keep in the lane when it takes a sharp right turn and leave it to go through a gate. Turn left and follow the wall on your left, leading you to a gate into another lane, soon to follow Dicks Beck downhill.

The path, among trees, crosses the beck and immediately you have a choice. Either cross a low fence and recross the stream into a woodland glade, soon to come to the main stream of Timble Gill Beck which, when not in spate, may be easily crossed on stones to a wet, enclosed lane; or go over a stile on the left to cross the corner of a field to another stile (waymarked) and a footbridge over the main stream. On the other side go downstream for less than 50 yards to turn uphill left into the wet lane. This much-used path, somewhat muddy at times and somewhat overgrown (but always passable), twists and turns until it joins another lane at a public footpath signpost. Turn left and take the lane on the right, past the second house, to the *Timble Inn*.

Return to the back lane and pass the signpost 'Public Footpath to Dobpark' (used before), now on the right. Fifty yards beyond it is another finger-post, on the left, indicating a public footpath to Swinsty Hall along a green lane. Take it. Pass through two gates, the second one with an adjoining ladder stile, going into an open field, and now keep on the track which bears left to a line of trees to follow a rough wall side and a stream to the edge of Swinsty Moor Plantation. Turn left along the edge, passing a small building within. The track soon enters the wood through a gate, 100 yards beyond which it forks, both branches joining again near the road. When last here, using a 1:25,000 map, we decided to take the right-hand path which was shown as passing through a tarn (this part of the woodland area is called Tarn Hill), but it was a dry passage through heather and gorse between trees, emerging at the car park. No doubt the tarn disappeared when the trees were planted.

9.   **5.5 miles**

Thruscross Reservoir
and Rocking Hall

ALL within the parish of Thruscross, today's walk on Rocking Moor is designed to give a breath of fresh moorland air to those not wishing to cover a great mileage, but who nevertheless seek a varied upland walk. Thruscross, the newest of the Washburn reservoirs, lends additional colour inasmuch as sailing is allowed; the return journey, especially, is enriched by the sight of the gay hues of the sails of the dinghies. The outward trip substantially follows part of the Harrogate Dalesway, which goes from Harrogate to Bolton Abbey where it joins the Dales Way. Devised by the Ramblers' Association West Riding Area, the original Dales Way starts at Ilkley and finishes at Bowness-on-Windermere, following on the way the rivers Wharfe, Dee and Kent.

It is opportune to quote from the publication of the Harrogate R.A. group of October 1974: *The route across Rocking Moor is on a public Access Area, not a public right-of-way. The Byelaws of the Barden Fell Access Agreement made between the West Riding County Council and the Trustees of the Chatsworth Settlement must be scrupulously observed. Note in particular that DOGS MUST NOT BE TAKEN INTO THE ACCESS AREA and camping is FORBIDDEN. The Estate gamekeepers and National Park Wardens will help you find your way. However, access may be restricted on a limited number of weekdays during the shooting season from the 12th August to 10th December, also in exceptional circumstances such as severe fire risk. Notices are posted at the public access points. To check that it will be clear on the day you intend to walk, telephone the Estate Office, Bolton Abbey 227.*

Parking: From the crossroads at Blubberhouses, motor northwards on the minor road signposted to West End. After two miles join the road coming in from the left from Bolton Abbey, continue past the modern church on the left for 300 yards downhill and park the car near the turn on the right (down to Thruscross Reservoir) (GR:144577).

On the left, before the side road, is a stile. Go over it and cross the field, keeping roughly to the wall on the right, initially, then make for the far corner to the top end of the broken wall on the left. Continue walking uphill, with a wall on the right, pass through a gate opening and keep straight on to the next gate, making for the building on the skyline (Baud Shaw). On the left the scene opens out, the church and the reservoir being prominent. Take the gateway at the top left-hand corner of the field, skirt to the left of the barn and go towards the wall on the left, then through a gateway, and immediately turn right for a few paces to another gate on to the road. Turn right for 20 yards to a footpath sign and gate on the right. Here is a notice 'No dogs allowed' being part of the Bolton Abbey Estate. Turn right, noting Burnt House to the left front, now on the Harrogate Dales Way.

Continue as far as Spittle Ings Farm, following the track to

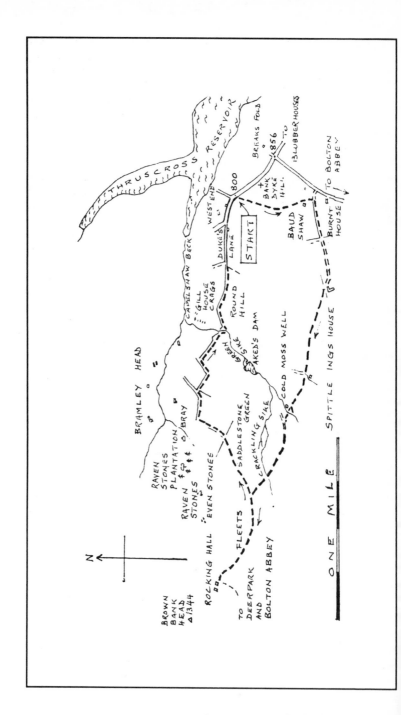

the right of it, through a gate in the wall, now to arrive on a fine moorland road. Straight ahead, on the skyline, the objective, Rocking Hall, should be in sight and our track should take us there without any difficulty or deviation. It becomes a grassy, tufty track and sometimes seems a long uphill slog, but this is moorland walking at its best. When an open green space is reached (Fleets), see another green track going back to the right — which is to be taken on your return. Pass into a compound and on to Rocking Hall where you will be greeted by a headstone above an arch. Between the 'Hall' and a farm building is a rocking stone — only now it seems to be wedged. Here is a good picnic place. Earl's Seat and Simon's Seat should be seen to the north; beyond Thruscross Reservoir and to the right of it are tall buildings in Harrogate; further to the right is the radio mast on Norwood Edge; then Beamsley Beacon, behind which are Otley Chevin and Ilkley Moor — identified by the twin television masts. Keighley Moor is further south and west; the Land-Rover route through a gate out of the compound towards it is a clear track leading to Bolton Abbey.

From Rocking Hall retrace your steps for half a mile to the second widening of the green track (there is a small heap of stones on the right), and bear left on grass through heather, leaving the outward route. Keep on in the same general direction, the path being sometimes quite plain, sometimes through bracken, sometimes narrow, but avoid other tracks leading away from the main route. Pick up a grassy path through the heather, bearing slightly right to a gate in, and a ladder stile over a crossing wall and continue forward with the remains of a very old wall and a new fence on the left. Go over another ladder stile to meet another wall at which turn right. A smooth grassy track takes you to a gate. Go through it. Turn right on the other side to another gate, back to the open moor. Keep to the moor side with the wall zig-zagging on the left, cross a ditch which goes underground and go through a gate into an open pasture. Still on the right of the wall, arrive at three gates, select the one on the right so as to continue forward, and then you will soon descend to Green Syke on a sunken path. Cross the stream — a good crossing is upstream on a stone below a pool (which is also inviting on a hot day) — and return to the wall side, following it up the moor. At the top of Round Hill the church on Bank Dyke Hill comes into sight. Leave the moor through a gate, which leads to Dukes Lane and to 200 yards of tarmac road downhill to the car.

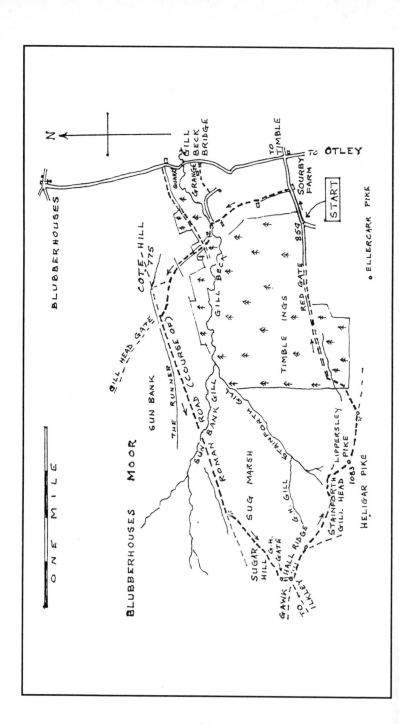

BLUBBERHOUSES

BLUBBERHOUSES MOOR

N

ONE MILE

GILL HEAD GATE

COTE HILL 775

SUN BANK

THE RUNNER (COURSE OF)

SUN ROAD (COURSE OF)

ROMAN BANK GILL

STAINFORTH GILL

GILL BECK

QUARRY

GRANGE

GILL BECK BRIDGE

TO TIMBLE

TO OTLEY

SOURBY FARM

START

850

RED GATE

TIMBLE INGS

ELLERCARR PIKE

SUG MARSH

SUGAR HILL G.H.

GAWK HALL GATE

TO ILKLEY

HALL RIDGE

G.H. GILL

STAINFORTH GILL HEAD

LIPPERSLEY PIKE 1063

HELIGAR PIKE

Blubberhouses Moor

MUCH fun was made on a succession of BBC1 Nationwide programmes about Blubberhouses, some suggesting there could be no such name. To many in the North, however, the name conjures up the beginnings of magic, wild places. The sudden appearance of the little village, with its church spire, Fewston Reservoir in front, and the circle of hills behind, has stirred the hearts of generations of travellers from the direction of Harrogate.

But it is not the village we shall visit today, but the moor of the same name, as we walk along the course of a Roman road to the Gawk Hall Ridge, and back by Lippersley Pike, finishing through the woods on Timble Ings.

Parking: On the Otley road, less than one-and-a-half miles from Blubberhouses is a road to Timble with a track opposite. Cars may use the track up to the junction signposted to Ellercar Pike and to Ilkley, where one may safely park (GR:165529).

Return on foot to Sourby Farm and go over a stone step stile opposite. Walk downhill with a wall on your left. Take the right-hand of two gates, or the stone step stile between, to continue downhill through the next field, with a wall on the left. Enter the paddock of an uninhabited farm, leaving it by a gate on the right to continue in your line of march, with a broken wall on the left.

At the foot of the next field, go over a stile to the right of a gate. Continue downhill with a wall and hedge on your left to a stile, taking you into a lane. Cross a lane into the next field, turn left by the side of a wall to pass to the right of some dilapidated farm buildings and down to Gill Beck. Some 100 yards downstream from the wall go through a gate to a wooden footbridge. Cross it and turn left to go upstream on a track through trees, which soon turns uphill to pass to the left of a dilapidated building, curling round it to the right to take you to a waymarked stile. Over it, cross a metalled forestry road to join a wide grassy track through woodland.

We are now on an ancient path known as Gill Head gate. Pass through a gate into a field and continue, with a wall on the left, to another gate and the open moor. You could keep to the main track of Gill Head Gate as far as the water cut 'The Runner' where you turn left along its bank or on the site of the Roman road, the green track a few yards before it. The spur of Cote Hill is, however, on the right and is inviting. Should you feel like accepting the invitation, leave the main path about 200 yards from the gate and go forward on indistinct tracks through the heather, to the ford at the foot of the hill which is at the turning of the water cut. Now go up the hill on a clear track (along which we shall return) to the highest point for a very fine view. To the north can be seen the farms on Hardisty Hill outside Blubberhouses — on the way to Thruscross. To the south-west is the route of the Roman road, which we joined at the foot of the hill, on the immediate left of The Runner. The highest point seen to the right of the Roman road is Black Fell (Round Hill on most maps) and, in clear conditions, you should see the upright post on Gawk Hall Ridge, the next high point, slightly to the left of the line of the Roman road.

Return and cross The Runner. Follow it upstream on springy turf through the heather. As you walk, look to the left for the return route over Lippersley Ridge and pause for a backward look at Fewston Reservoir. The stream at first is quite fast flowing and makes a pleasant sound. After about half a mile of walking beside it, look across Sun Bank Gill ahead and on the other side see the course of the Roman road marked by the brownish green reeds in another water cut on the right of it. From this point The Runner is veering almost imperceptibly to the right, hugging the side of Sun Bank. Leave it to go straight forward to cross Sun Bank Gill — a sheltered place, suitable for lunch. Continue uphill to walk beside the reeds in the water course on the slight embankment of the Roman road for 800 yards beyond the stream crossing and look for a low heap of stones in the heather on the left. This is where the Gawk Hall Gate path leaves the line of the Roman road; it is a faint green path through the heather pointing towards the upright post on Gawk Hall Ridge. Sometimes the path is lost in bog, water cuts or bracken, but it can usually be picked up beyond the obstacle and it becomes very clear as it approaches the gate in the wall at the foot of the ridge below the post. This gateway is marked on the 1:25,000 map at Gawk Hall Gate, but the writers are inclined to the view that the whole of the route we have recently been taking should carry the name. From the gateway, go up to the post on the ridge on a clear track to the right of the wall. A new scene is now before you, Rombalds

Moor being the main feature. The wooden finger-post (without arms) is fixed to an ancient upright stone on which is inscribed '12 M to RIPPON' with a finger pointing towards the Roman road and, pointing the other way, 'ILKLEY 3 M'. On a boulder at the gate through the wall on the ridge is carved '12 K F 1767'. Go over a ladder stile beside this gate and along the ridge on a clear path. The next objective — Lippersley Pike — should be seen ahead. 400 yards beyond the gate, keep left at a cairn (the narrow path to the right goes towards Heligar Pike). Descend to Stainforth Gill Head, where the track tends to be lost in marshy land, but it becomes clear when it bears to the right, ascending to Lippersley Pike, recognised by a substantial shelter (or butt), a cairn and a boundary stone on which is inscribed '11 KF 1767'. This, also, is a good viewpoint, Ilkley, Burley and Otley all being in sight.

Walk along Lippersley Ridge, slightly downhill as far as a cairn and an upright boundary stone marked 'D'. Bear left where the track forks to a ladder stile. On the other side, cross to a second stile to a clear narrow path in a plantation, soon to cross a stream to another stile over a wire fence. Turn right to continue with the fence on your right and young trees on each side. At a gate, turn right into a wide forest walk — Red Gate — which unerringly leads to the car after a quarter of mile.

11.   4.25 miles

Denton Moor

THE moors north of Ilkley and Otley towards Timble and Blubberhouses have long been favourites with walkers from Leeds and Bradford. Across them pass some ancient routes, many of which are still discernible — two will be used today — others, passing through boggy ground, are more difficult to find.

Instead of the selected starting point, the walk could begin from the direction of Timble. This would add a mile each way if starting from the crossroads near Sourby Farm, or if the car

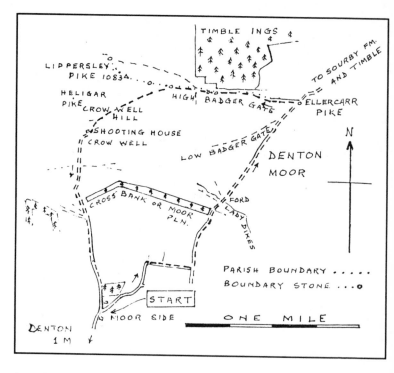

is taken past the farm to the signpost indicating to the left
'Public bridleway Ellercarr Pike', (GR:165529), the distance
added is only half a mile each way. Follow this good farm
road to the Pike — its highest point — (good views of Lindley
Wood Reservoir are on the way). Where the road turns sharply
to the right, go straight on through a gate or over a stile and
immediately turn right, and take up the circuit as described.

Those motoring from Ilkley or Otley on the Askwith/Middleton
road north of the river, turn north at the road junction to Denton
and on entering the village, bear left at the very fine stone, in
the shape of a font, and travel for a mile on the narrow tarmac
road (not shown as tarred on some maps) and park the car just
past Moorside Farm (GR:141505).

From Moorside Farm walk on the rough road on the right,
marked 'Public Footpath', passing in front of a new house and
to the right of a wood. Soon, square to the left, Beamsley Beacon
will come into sight; straight ahead is Cross Bank or Moor
Plantation. Turn right at the end of the road, as directed by a
public footpath sign, keep to the lower end of the field, with

a fence on the right, pass through a gate and continue forward, still with a fence on the right. Go through a gate and turn left on to a green cart track. There is a fine view across Wharfedale to the Guiseley Gap from the gateway. The track goes through another field and on to rough grassy moorland before passing the end of Moor Plantation, reaching open heather moors at Denton Moor on the other side of a high wooden stile.

At the stile, go forward slightly to the right to cross a ford over the little Lady Dikes, ignoring a footbridge 25 yards upstream to the left. Now follow a main track up the moor, walking alongside a ditch and stream. Away to the right the shooting house should be seen on Askwith Moor. Three hundred yards before coming to the highest point, a faint path comes in from the left. This is Low Badger Gate, the alternative — almost extinct — of the old pedlars' route from Langbar to Timble. Keep going forward to Ellercarr Pike, where walkers from Sowerby Farm join the circuit, but do not go through the gate (the road to Timble). Turn left as directed by a signpost 'Public footpath Middleton' (other directions are to Denton and to Timble). Now we are on the famous High Badger Gate track, green, through heather, with a wall on the right. Away to the right, across the Vale of York, the White Horse on the Hambleton Hills may be seen. This is moorland walking at its best. Keep to the main track parallel to the wall, making for Lippersley Ridge. Pass a cross track opposite the end of the plantation on Timble Ings and come to another cross track, cairn and boundary stone with a 'D' (for Denton) inscribed upon it. This is on Lippersley Ridge where the High Badger gate path bears away to the left, but it is worth continuing along the ridge to Lippersley Pike and returning to our track after admiring the view. On the top are a well-shaped shelter, a cairn and a boundary stone on which the following lettering appears: 'II KF 1767'. Ilkley, Burley and Otley are all in sight. Moor Plantation is again seen and our path is to go past the right-hand edge of it.

Return to the High Badger Gate track over Crow Well Hill, to the left of Heligar Pike — butts on your right point the general direction — and, leaving High Badger Gate, go in front of the shooting house at Crow Well. Continue downhill with butts on your right and then on your left. The route of the Low Badger Gate path, difficult to find, crosses our path as we continue downhill on the main trail, passing to the left of the end of the belt of trees to a metalled track which goes through gates and soon reaches Moor Side.

12.

'A' route: 5 miles
'B' route: 6.5 miles
'C' route: 2.75 miles

Middleton Moor
and Beamsley Beacon

IN this walk we shall explore the main feature north of Ilkley — Beamsley Beacon and the hills associated with it. Walkers on the suggested 'B' route will take in the ridge through the Old Pike to Black Fell (Round Hill) or, if you would prefer a lower return, route 'A' through Langbar is offered. For those not wishing to make the final ascent, but who are looking for a short walk on Middleton Moor, the 'C' route has been devised. All the walks touch the western end of the old pedlars' tracks — High and Low Badger Gate.

Parking: The starting point is just north of Ling Park where there is room for several cars to park on the roadside (GR:106504).

Walk along the road to a track at the corner of Ling Park Plantation. On the track, curve round to the wall side and follow this to the concrete square at the junction of tracks. Here go acutely left across grass, roughly bisecting the angle of the walls, making for the twin tops of Beamsley Beacon on open moorland. This is Low Badger Gate, which passes over the low Delves and Middle Ridges and drops down to Drya Dikes where stepping stones cross bog and beck. A paved trod then leads up to a direction stone at the junction of the High and Low Badger Gate routes, marked on the approach side of the stone 'To Skipton' and this is the track to be taken by 'A' and 'B' parties. (Forward, the single track is known as Badgers Gate.)

Long Ridge is to the left, Foldshaw Ridge to the right. Walkers on 'C' route would be rewarded by good views of Addingham and beyond by going to the top of Long Ridge before returning to follow High Badger Gate along the Foldshaw Ridge, and leaving it to turn right at the wall and right again at the high stile where you rejoin the outward track. Follow this track back to the concrete square and the car.

'A' and 'B' walkers go forward on Badgers Gate, passing through a gate and following a wall on the left to Wards End

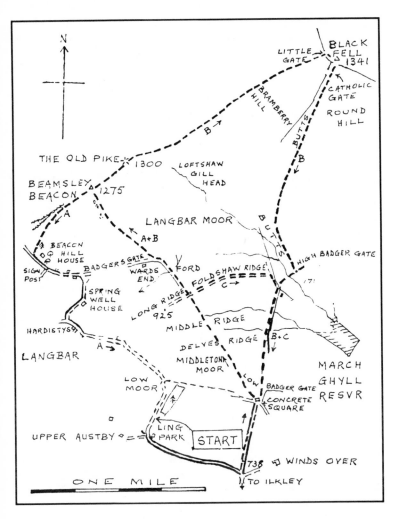

Farm from which Badgers Gate continues by the wall side towards
Langbar. But leave it just before Wards End to climb diagonally
uphill on a green track through bracken. A clear single track
which leads upwards towards the Beacon may be lost in bracken
near the top, but it may be picked up again to the right of some
rocks. Just before reaching the cairn at the Beacon, a wide
gritty path coming up from the left will be seen. This is the
return route for 'A' party, but before taking it some may wish
to take the track to the right to the higher top — The Old Pike
— a quarter of a mile away.

The aspect from both tops is superb. The vast panorama includes Chelker Reservoir below, backed by Draughton and Skipton Moors and a superb view of Bolton Abbey among the trees to the north-east with Upper Wharfedale stretching northwards from it, flanked, in the distance, by Buckden Pike and Old Cote Moor.

The 'B' party track passes the cairn on the Old Pike and snakes across Beamsley Moor on the left and Langbar Moor on the right, parish boundary stones on the way being suitably marked with a 'B' and 'LN' (the 'N' to show that the parish is Langbar with Nesfield). This is also the National Park boundary. After a mile of walking over the open moor, the path gently ascends Bramberry Hill to a gap in a wall — Little Gate. Go through it and turn right to the cairn on Black Fell 200 yards away. Return to the wall, passing through the next gate and continue forward with a wall on your right. The first gateway in that wall is Catholic Gate but do not go through it. Instead, keep descending, gradually leaving the wall and following a line of shooting butts. The double track joins another line of butts before Loftshaw Gill; follow it down to a gate in a cross fence. Turn right on the High Badger gate track, cross the stream, after which the Badger Gate route bears right, but leave it to go forward to a high wooden stile. Follow the good wide track forward to rejoin the outward route at the concrete square and the outward track to the car.

From Beamsley Beacon, 'A' party turns downhill on the wide path which goes to the right of the trees surrounding Beacon Hill House. Turn left on the tarmac road but, instead of following it downhill after 200 yards, go forward, passing a signpost 'Ilkley 4; Bolton Abbey two-and-three-quarters' on a private road. This is the beginning of Badgers Gate. Pass houses and buildings and reach an open area on the right. Go down through reeds and pass to the right of Spring Well House on a gravel road, turning left on regaining the tarmac road. Proceed past Hardisty's Farm and continue on the road uphill to Moor End Farm. Here the road turns sharply right on to open moorland for half a mile, with a good grass verge, to arrive at Ling Park Plantation and the car.

Bolton Priory
and Hazlewood Moor

BOLTON ABBEY is a famous place. Surely most Yorkshire folk have explored the priory, looked through the 'Hole in the Wall', crossed the river by the stepping stones or sturdy footbridge and walked through the woods upstream to the Strid. Here is the dividing point between Upper and Lower Wharfedale. Much of its beauty lies in its setting; the rippling Wharfe in pastoral and woodland surroundings; the colourful moors in the background. It is from the moors that the best aspects may be seen. Beamsley and Hazlewood Moors, visited today, should give the walker memorable views.

Parking: About half a mile north of Bolton Abbey village, take the track to the right, just before Cavendish Memorial, which leads to the car park near the Cavendish Pavilion (GR:077553). A charge is made.

Walk across the Wooden Bridge and go forward up the lane, crossing the tarmac road into another lane at the foot of which is a notice on a tree advertising accommodation at Bolton Park Farm (Phone Bolton Abbey 244). You are now in the Barden Moor and Fell Access area which is sometimes closed to the public for shooting. When visited early in September a notice was displayed giving dates when access was to be restricted. Assuming no restriction, continue up the gravel road and pass in front of Park House, then through an iron gate and another one into the park, following a tractor trail which goes uphill beside Stead Dike and continues on a stony track to a wide wooden gate. Look back for views of Bolton Abbey and the two cairns on Beamsley Beacon. Still climbing, Hammerthorne Gate is reached and beside it is a substantial stile over the wall and a 'no dogs' notice. The major track bears to the left, but leave it here to go forward on a double track with a green centre, leaving the wall. Now we are on heather moor at over 1,000 feet, passing the track which goes to the left over Long Ridge to Rocking Moor (see Walk 9). Our track turns right and eventually goes downhill to a ford through Pickles Gill Beck. Here also is a charming waterfall.

Continue on the good double track, heathery and grassy, passing

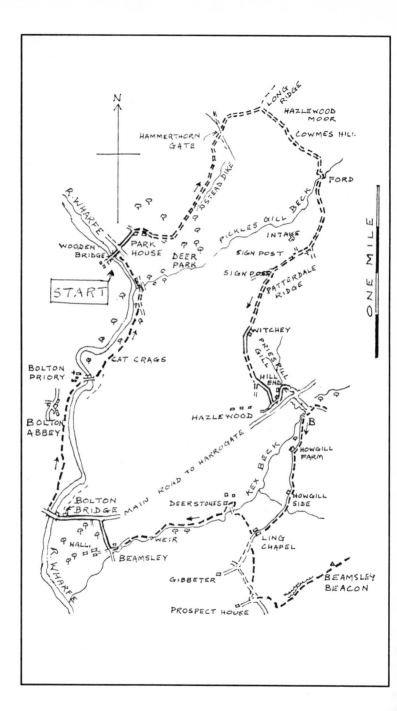

an intake and old ruined building down on the right. Views towards Skipton and beyond are to the right front. Ignoring a turn-off to the left, with a triangular link, go 75 yards further on to a signpost which reads 'Access Area' and 'Storiths' (the track to the right goes down to Intake Farm). Follow the Storiths track. From here is a view of Lower Barden Reservoir, behind which are the rocks and monuments on Cracoe and Rylstone Moors. Uphill, forward, the track soon comes to another signpost, from which, looking back, the twin tops of Simon's Seat (with trig point) and Lord's Seat should be seen. The signpost indicates 'Storiths' to the right but keep to the trail straight on (which is not indicated on the signpost). The two cairns on Beamsley Beacon should now be seen to the left front, with Ilkley and Addingham Moors beyond. Pass to the right of the farm at Witchey and through a gate where the surface becomes suitable for traffic to the farm. Five hundred yards further on, the wall on the left bears away from the metalled road. Take the green track by the side of it to enter a high-walled green lane which joins the narrow tarmac road from Hazlewood.

Bear left and continue past the buildings of Hill End. Cross the bridge on the old road and continue to the new A59. Cross this busy main road to a gate opposite and go down the sloping tarmac track to join the grassy lane to Kex Beck, which cross on a substantial footbridge. Take the track past Howgill Farm and Howgill Side to Ling Chapel Farm. Having just passed it you may be tempted to climb to Beamsley Beacon which is at the top of the hill on the left. The climb and return would add a mile and a half to the journey but on a clear day the prospect would be worth it. At Ling Chapel turn downhill and go through a wooden gate with a footpath signpost pointing to Dearstones, to join a path curling steeply down to a footbridge over Kex Beck in a delightful ravine. Bend uphill to Deerstones and on reaching the first house, take the track to the left of it to go downstream, with the ravine on the left and a wall on the right. Go over a stile on the left of a gate and, continuing with a wall on the right, go down to the water and keep by the waterside until reaching a broken weir near a large farm building. Cross over a stile in the wall on the right and cross the field to a stile at the far corner, then to an embankment between the stream and the mill race. Cross a footbridge over the mill race and climb a stone stile into a lane to come to Beamsley, with its creeper-covered houses. Turn right on the narrow tarmac road, then left at the main road to walk on the roadside footpath, with the parkland of Beamsley Hall on the left. Cross Bolton

Bridge and go through a little gate on the right at which there is a collecting box, this being part of the Chatsworth Estate. Now take the Dales Way path through the riverside fields to Bolton Abbey.

After loitering at the priory, cross the footbridge or the stepping stones and take the track sloping upwards, left, through the woods at Cat Crags. Join the tarmac road from Storiths, pass over Pickles Gill Beck on a footbridge beside the water splash and go over a stile on the left. Walk on the riverside to another stile, the Wooden Bridge and the car or the Cavendish Pavilion where refreshments are usually served.

Bolton Priory